Biofuels

Biofuels

Christopher Bahn

Living in THE FUTURE

CREATIVE EDUCATION
CREATIVE PAPERBACKS

Published by Creative Education and Creative Paperbacks
P.O. Box 227, Mankato, Minnesota 56002
Creative Education and Creative Paperbacks are imprints
of The Creative Company
www.thecreativecompany.us

Book design by Blue Design (www.bluedes.com)
Art direction by Graham Morgan
Edited by Barbara Ciletti

Photographs by Getty Images/James MacDonald/Bloomberg, 30, JEAN-FRANCOIS MONIER, 17, JESUSDEFUENSANTA, 19, Laurent MAOUS, 2, Nicholas Kajoba/Xinhua News Agency, 41, Patrick Pleul/picture alliance, 26, PUNIT PARANJPE, 13, Sirisak Boakaew, 20, Yang Zhili/VCG, 38; Pexels/Alejandro Barrón, 10, Engin Akyurt, cover, 6–7, Tomáš Malík, 4–5, Vlad Bagacian, 9; Shutterstock/Kletr, 37; Unsplash/Andrey Andreyev, 44, Christina Maïia, 34, Liz Harrell, cover, Matthew, 14; Wikimedia Commons/Curimedia, 33, Forest and Kim Starr, 29, published by Randolph Ackermann, 23, Tiia Monto, 45, William Creswell, 25

Every effort has been made to contact copyright holders for material reproduced in this book. Any omissions will be rectified in subsequent printings if notice is given to the publisher.

Copyright © 2026 Creative Education, Creative Paperbacks
International copyright reserved in all countries.
No part of this book may be reproduced in any form without written permission from the publisher.

Library of Congress Cataloging-in-Publication Data
Names: Bahn, Christopher (Children's story writer) author
Title: Biofuels / Christopher Bahn.
Description: Mankato, Minnesota : Creative Education and Creative Paperbacks, [2026] | Series: Living in the future | Includes bibliographical references and index. | Audience: Ages 10-14 | Audience: Grades 7-9 | Summary: "Explore how organic materials can be converted into clean energy. This book explains the science behind biofuels and their potential to reduce our reliance on fossil fuels. Written for middle-grade readers, it includes real-life examples of energy use, sidebars, a glossary, and an index"— Provided by publisher.
Identifiers: LCCN 2025015982 (print) | LCCN 2025015983 (ebook) | ISBN 9798895811207 library binding | ISBN 9798896800736 paperback | ISBN 9798895812464 ebook
Subjects: LCSH: Biomass energy—Juvenile literature
Classification: LCC TP339 .B325 2026 (print) | LCC TP339 (ebook) | DDC 662/.88—dc23/eng/20250612
LC record available at https://lccn.loc.gov/2025015982
LC ebook record available at https://lccn.loc.gov/2025015983

Printed in the United States

CONTENTS

Old-School Biofuel 8

Chapter 1: How Biofuels Work 11
    ZOOM IN: GREEN GOALS 14
    ZOOM IN: WATT DO YOU MEAN? 16

Chapter 2: History of Biofuels 18
    ZOOM IN: DON'T MAKE LIKE A TREE AND LEAVE 21
    ZOOM IN: CARS AND BIOFUELS 24

Chapter 3: Biofuels Today 27
    ZOOM IN: A KERNEL OF DOUBT 28
    ZOOM IN: WHEN "MOO" MEANS METHANE 34

Chapter 4: The Future of Biofuel 36
    ZOOM IN: KELP MIGHT HELP 38
    ZOOM IN: BIOFUELS IN SCI-FI 43

Getting Real: 44
    TRADITIONAL BIOFUELS 44
    BIOMASS POWER PLANTS 45

Timeline 46

Websites 46

Glossary 47

Selected Bibliography 47

Index 48

Old-School Biofuel

Have you ever warmed yourself by the heat of a campfire, toasting marshmallows and trading spooky stories in the dark? Then you have used biofuel. Simply defined, a biofuel is any kind of energy made from something living. Wood, when burned in a fire, is a classic example. Humans have been burning wood to produce heat and light for over one million years, making biofuels the oldest renewable energy source.

Today, biofuels are a vital part of the world's total energy supply. Billions of people around the world still rely on traditional wood fires as their main energy source for cooking and heating their homes. But people also use biofuels in far more technologically advanced ways to power civilization—chiefly to make electricity and to fuel cars, trucks, planes, and other forms of transport. These biofuels include ethanol, a corn-based gasoline additive, and biodiesel, a petroleum alternative made from vegetable oil or animal fat. If used wisely, biofuels could help society transition away from dangerous, climate-altering fossil fuels and into a future dominated by clean and renewable energy sources.

Plants capture energy from the sun, which we then are able to transform into biofuels.

CHAPTER 1:

How Biofuels Work

Energy is central to human civilization. Modern society requires vast amounts of energy to function, and we have built enormous, complex systems to generate and distribute that energy.

Continent-spanning networks of power lines connect our cities, homes, hospitals, and schools. Thousands of miles of roads carry millions of cars and trucks. Trains, airplanes and cargo ships criss-cross the world. Our energy network runs largely on fossil fuels such as coal, oil, and gas. But these fuels are expensive, polluting, and contribute to **global warming**—and they will eventually be used up. It is increasingly important to find alternative energy sources, including solar, wind, hydropower, geothermal, nuclear power, and the topic of this book, biofuels.

Biofuels are fuels made from living organisms, such as plants and animals. Think of biofuels as stored sunlight—plants capture solar energy through **photosynthesis**, converting it into sugars, which we then transform into biofuels.

Biomass, the raw material used to produce biofuels, comes from a variety of sources, including food crops such as wheat, corn, and sugarcane, which are grown for human and animal consumption. These sources are known as biofuel feedstocks. Oil-rich plants like canola and palm also serve as key feedstocks. In addition, agricultural waste, including inedible rice husks, sugarcane stalks, and animal manure, can be repurposed for fuel production. Wood byproducts, such as sawdust and bark from lumber mills, further contribute to biomass resources, along with municipal waste like garbage and sewage. Non-edible energy crops, such as willow, elephant grass, and switchgrass, offer a promising alternative, as they grow quickly, cost less, and often have a smaller environmental impact than food-based biofuel sources.

When biomass is burned to generate heat for transportation fuels or electricity, the process is called **bioenergy**. When it is processed into solid, liquid, or gas fuels, it becomes a biofuel. These fuels can be used on their own or blended with fossil fuels to power cars, trucks, airplanes, and even electricity-generating turbines.

Biofuels are used in several ways. In 2020, biomass accounted for about 10% of the world's total energy consumption—mostly by direct combustion—burning it—for home cooking and heating. Biomass is also used to heat industrial facilities and power steam turbines that generate electricity.

A compressed biogas plant in India uses bales of leftover rice plant material.

ZOOM IN: GREEN GOALS

To replace fossil fuels, alternative energy must be renewable, sustainable, and carbon neutral. Biofuels come from regrowing crops, so they are renewable. But they still have problems with sustainability and carbon emissions. Researchers are working to improve them, but biofuels are not perfect yet.

Biomass undergoes several chemical processes to be converted into usable fuels in solid, liquid, or gas forms. Biological conversion includes fermentation, where crops like corn are transformed into ethanol—a liquid fuel blended with gasoline to reduce oil dependence, lower costs, and cut emissions. Another method, **anaerobic** digestion, mirrors natural digestion, breaking down organic waste in sealed tanks to produce biogas, primarily methane and carbon dioxide, which can be used as natural gas or converted into syngas, a gasoline-like fuel. Thermal conversion involves heating biomass to extremely high temperatures in sealed chambers, sometimes with steam or gases like hydrogen or oxygen, generating fuels such as charcoal, bio-oil, methane, and hydrogen gas, along with renewable alternatives to diesel, gasoline, and jet fuel that do not rely on fossil fuels.

Biomass is also a source of energy for humans—we consume it as food. This has made biofuels controversial. Cultivating biomass often competes directly with food production. Crops grown for biofuels could instead feed hungry people. For example, **sustainability** expert Mike Berners-Lee notes that the amount of wheat needed to fuel a Toyota Corolla for just 1.1 miles on bioethanol could feed a person for an entire day.

Biofuels are categorized into four generations based on their production methods. First-generation biofuels are derived from food crops like corn, sugarcane, and canola. The sugars and

Production of biofuels requires large crops.

HOW BIOFUELS WORK — 15

starches in these plants are turned into liquid hydrocarbons for use as fuel. This is controversial because those same food crops and the lands used to grow them are also in high demand for feeding humans.

Second-generation biofuels come from non-food plant materials such as straw and wood, reducing food competition but requiring significant land and complex processing.

Third-generation biofuels use algae, which have high oil content and can be cultivated in non-farmable areas like deserts or oceans.

Fourth-generation biofuels rely on genetically engineered organisms—such as microbes, yeast, and fungi—to capture carbon and produce biofuels more efficiently. However, both third- and fourth-generation biofuels are still in early development and not widely adopted.

Critics argue that first-generation biofuels take away food resources and farmland, while supporters believe careful planning can minimize these issues. Many experts see biofuels as just one piece of a larger energy puzzle, alongside solar and wind power. Unlike solar and wind, which depend on the weather, biofuels offer a reliable energy source that can be stored as a dry solid, liquid, or gas and used whenever needed.

ZOOM IN: WATT DO YOU MEAN?

Energy use is commonly measured in watts, indicating the power needed for a task—like a 40-watt bulb requiring 40 watts to shine. Power plants track output in watt-hours (Wh), with larger units including megawatt-hours (MWh) (1 million Wh) and terawatt-hours (TWh) (1 million MWh). In 2023, bioethanol and biodiesel produced 1,200 TWh, a huge jump from 100 TWh in 1990, though fossil fuels still dominated with 140,000 TWh in the same year.

Wood pellets are used as a second-generation biofuel, but require complex processing.

HOW BIOFUELS WORK — 17

CHAPTER 2:

History of Biofuels

> Ancient humans used biofuels in their fires and to draw on cave walls.

Biofuels are far from a modern invention. The use of fire as an energy source dates back over a million years, long before modern humans even existed. In fact, many scientists believe that mastering fire was a crucial milestone in human evolution. Fire provided warmth, protection from predators, and a means to cook food, all of which helped early humans survive and thrive. Some argue that the controlled use of fire was the single most important invention in human history, forming the foundation for all future technological advancements.

One of the earliest biofuels was charcoal, created by heating wood in a low-oxygen, high-temperature kiln. Humans used charcoal at least 30,000 years ago to draw on cave walls, and by 4000 BCE, it became vital for metalworking, ushering in the Bronze and Iron Ages. By 900 CE, Chinese alchemists

ZOOM IN: DON'T MAKE LIKE A TREE AND LEAVE

Humans have cleared forests for farming and grazing since prehistory, but **deforestation** sped up as populations grew—especially during the Industrial Age. Today, agriculture drives most forest loss, destroying over 50 million hectares of tropical rainforests in the last decade. Deforestation fuels climate change, causing about 20% of global **greenhouse gas** emissions, and disrupts the water cycle, indigenous rights, and biodiversity. Expanding biofuel crops, which need large land areas, raises concerns and drives research into next-generation biofuels to lower environmental impact.

Biofuels may increase deforestation through either the use of firewood or the development of large crop fields.

---

discovered that charcoal was a key ingredient in gunpowder, forever altering warfare and technology.

Throughout history, people have used other organic materials as fuel. Animal fats and vegetable oils such as olive oil have illuminated lamps for thousands of years—one of the earliest known lamps, found in France's Lascaux Cave, is 17,300 years old. The word oil itself comes from the Greek *elaia*, meaning olive.

Another ancient biofuel process is fermentation, which produces ethanol—the same substance found in alcoholic drinks like beer and wine. Brewing beer dates back 13,000 years in the Middle East, and by 1826, inventor Samuel Morey became the first to use ethanol to power an engine.

For most of human history, wood was the dominant fuel source. However, as populations grew and demand for firewood outpaced natural regrowth, deforestation became a major issue. By 1600, coal began replacing wood as the primary fuel in Europe and North America, and by the 20th century, it had taken over as the main energy source. Coal had several advantages: It was abundant and easy to mine, and it was more energy-dense, producing more heat per pound than wood.

The Industrial Revolution further accelerated the shift. In the 18th century, James Watt's steam engine transformed civilization, making mass production and mechanized transportation possible. While Watt's machine ran on coal, its design was inspired by a much older biofuel-powered invention—the *aeolipile*, a steam-powered device created 2,000 years ago by the Greek-Egyptian mathematician Hero of Alexandria. Hero's device used wood fires to boil water, creating steam to turn a turbine.

Biofuels play a crucial role in history despite the use of coal. The demand for palm oil, an industrial lubricant made from oil-palm fruit, fueled European colonization of Africa in the 1800s. Today, palm oil remains a major global industry, especially in Indonesia, Malaysia, and Nigeria.

Whaling was another biofuel-based industry. During the 1700s and 1800s, whale oil became essential for lighting homes and lubricating industrial machinery. Ambergris, a substance from sperm whales, was used in perfumes and medicine, while baleen (whalebone) was a key material for corsets and umbrellas.

However, the whaling industry had devastating consequences. The blue whale population plummeted from 300,000 to around 10,000 due to overhunting. Even after petroleum replaced whale oil in the late 19th century, whaling continued—whale fat was used to make margarine, soap, and even explosives during the World Wars. Industrial whaling was finally banned in 1982, though some countries, including Norway, Japan, and Iceland, still allow small-scale whaling today.

The modern biofuel era began in the 1890s, when German inventor Rudolf Diesel developed a highly efficient engine powered by a new type of fuel—both of which now bear his name. While diesel

> The need fo whale oil created an entire whaling industry in the 1700 and 1800s..

fuel is usually petroleum-based, Diesel's original engine was able to run on vegetable oil. His innovation paved the way for modern biodiesel, which can be made from various vegetable and plant oils.

Despite this breakthrough, biofuels struggled to compete with petroleum-based fuels. After World War II, the global economy was powered by cheap and abundant fossil fuels, particularly from the Middle East. Petroleum dominated the energy industry and pushed biofuel to the sidelines for decades.

The 1970s oil crisis changed everything. A sudden petroleum shortage caused economic turmoil, prompting governments to explore alternative energy sources. Growing concerns about climate change further fueled interest in renewable biofuels.

The United States and Brazil emerged as pioneers in biofuel production, each leveraging their native crops to develop distinct approaches. The U.S. focused on corn-based ethanol, rapidly scaling up production in the 1980s, and by 2005, more than 100 ethanol plants were in operation nationwide. Meanwhile, Brazil turned to sugarcane ethanol, a biofuel it had been refining since the 1920s, utilizing its favorable climate and high-yield crops to establish a robust ethanol industry.

ZOOM IN:
CARS AND BIOFUELS

Automobiles are among the biggest consumers of fossil fuels today, but biofuel ethanol once rivaled gasoline in the early auto industry, backed by innovators like Alexander Graham Bell and Thomas Edison. Henry Ford designed the Model T to run on either fuel, calling ethanol "the fuel of the future." In 1925, he told *The New York Times* that ethanol could be made from apples, weeds, sawdust, and almost anything, even claiming that an acre of potatoes could yield enough alcohol to power farm machinery for a century.

The Model T could run on either ethanol or gasoline.

Although biofuels faced challenges—such as high production costs, limited infrastructure, and efficiency concerns—governments provided support. Between 1994 and 2009, the U.S. allocated nearly $6 billion in subsidies for biofuel research and development.

Since then, biofuel production has skyrocketed. By the mid-2000s, bioethanol and biodiesel output had increased more than 25-fold, making biofuels a key player in the global energy mix.

CHAPTER 3:

Biofuels Today

Over the past 50 years, biofuels have seen an impressive rise. In the United States, electricity made from biomass is now more than 45 times what it was in the 1980s, and global production is now 15 times higher. Today, biofuels produce about 2 percent of all electricity. They still pale compared to other power sources like fossil fuels, which make up more than half of the world's energy.

The United States, China, Brazil, and Germany lead in biofuel-based electricity, but some smaller countries also rely heavily on biomass. For example, while biofuels provide only about 5% of the U.S.'s electricity, Sweden generates nearly a quarter of its power from wood biomass. Sweden's abundant forests make this method practical, but in many regions, biofuel production is limited because farmland is primarily used for food.

The fermentation tanks of a biogas plant are where bacteria break down the organic matter and produce methane-rich biogas.

ZOOM IN: A KERNEL OF DOUBT

When it comes to American biofuels, corn is king. About 75 percent of all Midwestern farmland—about 180 million acres—is used to grow corn. About a quarter of that is used to make ethanol, which makes up 10 percent of the fuel used in cars. The U.S. makes about 15 billion gallons of corn ethanol every year. But is it ecologically sustainable? It takes a lot of resources to grow corn, including large amounts of fertilizer and pesticides.

Biofuels now supply about 10% of the world's total energy, but a large portion still comes from traditional wood-burning, which remains common in developing countries. In industrialized nations, bioenergy is a growing sector. Wood is also now used more efficiently in the form of wood pellets—compressed sawdust or low-quality forest wood—burned in furnaces and boilers for heat and electricity. These pellets produce less pollution and burn more efficiently than coal or natural gas.

The most widely used biofuels today are ethanol, biodiesel (or renewable diesel), biomethane, and bio-jet fuel. The U.S. produces about 15 billion gallons of ethanol each year, most of which is blended into gasoline. A common mixture, called E10, consists of 90% gasoline and 10% ethanol. This blend helps lower carbon

A worker delivers recycled cooking grease to a facility where it can be processed into biodiesel.

emissions and reduces dependence on foreign oil. Nearly 40% of all corn grown in the U.S. is used for ethanol production, and together with Brazil, these two countries produce 80% of the world's ethanol. Brazil has relied on sugarcane-based ethanol since the 1920s, thanks to its tropical climate.

Biodiesel is another major biofuel. Unlike traditional diesel made from petroleum, biodiesel can be produced from vegetable oils, animal fats, or even recycled cooking grease. Soybeans are the primary source in the U.S. In 2020, the country produced about 1.87 billion gallons of biodiesel, which can be used alone or blended with regular diesel. A related product, hydrotreated vegetable oil (also called renewable diesel), provides another cleaner alternative to petroleum-based diesel.

The majority of the methane— also known as natural gas—that we use comes from deep underground as a fossil fuel. However, methane can also be made as a biofuel in ways that are more environmentally friendly than drilling. For example, when trash in landfills breaks down, it produces methane and carbon dioxide. This gas can be captured by drilling boreholes as deep as 30 meters. Today, more than 500 such projects are operating in the U.S. Methane can also be gathered from livestock manure or human sewage. After it is cleaned, the gas is used for heating, generating electricity, or as fuel for vehicles. This process, called anaerobic digestion, happens naturally in compost piles and even in the stomachs of cows. (Yes, cows do release methane from their backsides! In fact, they make so much of it that cow's, er, emissions are responsible for about 5 percent of global warming.) In the developing world—especially in Asia—biogas is growing. About 30 million homes in China use biogas, while in sub-Saharan Africa, many people are instead turning to solar energy.

Despite these advances, most experts believe biofuels will never be the world's primary alternative energy source. Solar and wind power are widely seen as the most sustainable options, but they also have limitations. For example, wind and solar energy cannot easily replace liquid fuels like gasoline, diesel, and jet fuel. This is where biofuels are useful—when processed into methane or biodiesel, they work similarly to fossil fuels and can be used in existing engines and infrastructure.

Air travel, for example, is a major source of pollution, as jet fuel is a highly refined form of kerosene. Switching to bio-jet fuel could reduce emissions, but it remains costly. Bio-jet fuel is made from sources such as plant oils, algae, agricultural waste, and municipal waste. Yet, in 2018, less than 0.1% of all jet fuel came from biofuels, largely due to high production costs.

Other renewable energy sources cannot yet replace liquid fuel, whereas biofuels can.

ZOOM IN: WHEN "MOO" MEANS METHANE

Believe it or not, one of the most unexpected sources of biofuel comes from ... a cow's rear end! In 1808, British scientist Humphry Davy discovered that cow manure releases methane, a potent biofuel gas. As organic waste decomposes, it produces biogas, which can be captured and used as an energy source. In fact, as early as 1895, the city of Exeter, England, used methane from sewage to power street lamps.

One challenge with biofuels is the inefficiency of photosynthesis—plants convert only about 1% of sunlight into biomass. This means biofuel crops require large amounts of land. If Japan used all its farmland for biofuel production, it would only cover about 30% of its gasoline needs. The World Resources Institute estimates that solar panels generate over 100 times more energy per hectare than biofuels. However, biomass can be grown in areas unsuitable for food crops, such as deserts, or produced from waste materials like farm byproducts, lumber scraps, and municipal trash.

While these alternatives are more environmentally friendly than fossil fuels, it is tricky to make them work as full replacements. For one thing, biofuels must still be burned in the vehicle's engine, and so they still release carbon and contribute to global warming. Additionally, many biofuels cannot be used alone in standard gasoline engines without causing damage, so they must be blended with conventional fuels. Looking ahead, some experts believe solar-powered electric cars and hydrogen fuel cells may be the best long-term solution.

While biofuels may not be the ultimate answer to the world's energy challenges, they remain an important part of the transition to a cleaner, more sustainable future.

CHAPTER 4:

The Future of Biofuel

Biofuels could help with the world's energy problems, but there are significant challenges. While scientists have made progress, many new biofuel technologies are still not ready. There are also problems to solve, like pollution and competition with food production. Biofuels release fewer greenhouse gases than fossil fuels, but they are not completely clean.

Biofuels alone cannot replace fossil fuels, but they can help while we develop better energy sources like solar and wind power. They can also come from waste, like trash from landfills and leftover wood from logging. In the future, new plants could be grown just for biofuel, and better versions could be made for airplanes and

Biofuel plants are large facilities.

ZOOM IN: KELP MIGHT HELP

Although the idea of farming seaweed might seem strange, it has been a staple industry in Japan and Korea for centuries and expanded massively after the 1940s. Today, global production reaches 24 million tons annually, with projections of 500 million tons by 2050. Seaweed aquaculture has multiple uses—in food, medicine, cosmetics, and even habitat restoration—but its role in fighting climate change is especially exciting. It absorbs around 10% of the ocean's carbon emissions each year.

Harvest season on a Chinese kelp farm.

ships. Biomass could be a good solution for nations that do not have their own fossil fuel reserves, but do have agricultural land they can spare for biofuel crops. There are genuine concerns about biofuels, and not everyone thinks they will play a big role in future energy production. Bill Ritter, former governor of Colorado and author of Powering Forward, warns that biofuels are renewable but may not be clean or sustainable. Professor Mark Z. Jacobson, author of *No Miracles Needed*, argues that wind, solar, and hydropower are better because biofuels create pollution, contribute to climate change, and use too much land.

Biofuels' biggest advantage is their similarity to fossil fuels—they can be used as "drop-in fuels" in existing engines and furnaces. While experts like Oxford's Nick Jelley see solar-powered cars as the future, biofuels offer a practical transition in the meantime.

Biomass is more eco-friendly than fossil fuels in many ways: For one, it is renewable, since the plants harvested can grow again. But we will need to practice good land and water management, and lots of time: it may take 10 years for a savannah to regrow, and 80 years for a forest. Harvesting too many crops in search of profits can also be very bad, as seen on the Indonesian island of Borneo, where deforestation caused in part by palm-oil plantations has caused an ongoing crisis.

Burning biomass to create biofuels produces soot, which contributes to global warming and air pollution. In the future, we may be able to capture and store the carbon produced from power plants underground, cutting its overall impact on the climate. This process is called Carbon Capture and Storage. Scientists hope biomass will play a key role in this process, but more research is needed—it's still too expensive to be practical. The same potential applies to non-biofuel biomass, like the millions of tons of municipal garbage burned in incinerators each year.

Researchers are also trying to find better ways of working with "second-generation" biofuel feedstocks, which would be non-edible (and thus won't increase world hunger) or could grow in regions of the Earth that would make poor farmland. Second-generation fuels have not yet panned out as hoped but are thought to have great potential. Fast-growing switchgrass and poplar, as well as more exotic plants like jatropha and pongamia, are being looked at. And cactus might be ideal for making use of at least some of the world's 25 million square kilometers of desert and semi-arid land. (Although we still need to tread carefully about land overuse, since what may be "poor" for crops may still be important habitat for wildlife.)

"Third-generation" or algal biofuel, which is still not yet commercially successful, is made by cultivating microscopic plants called algae in large outdoor

Briquettes of agricultural waste are used as biofuel.

ponds to harvest their oily secretions, which are then made into "green crude", a petroleum alternative. (Seaweed in the ocean could also be cultivated this way.) Algae grow very fast and the ponds could be constructed in deserts using non-drinkable wastewater. Its greenhouse-gas footprint might be half as much as regular diesel. But the technology is quite a ways away from being ready, despite tens of millions of dollars spent on research so far.

We have learned how to change the nature of plants and animals at their most basic level.

ew advances in science have opened new horizons in biofuels. One of the most intriguing (and potentially dangerous) is genomics, the study of life's fundamental building block, DNA. We have learned how to change the nature of plants and animals at their most basic level. Using genetic modification, scientists hope to produce "fourth-generation" biofuels from new kinds of microbes, algae, and yeast that could be cheaper, cleaner, and more efficient, and may even be able to clean away pollution that's already in our air and water. One candidate is butanol, an ethanol alternative that might be produced using

> **ZOOM IN:**
> **BIOFUELS IN SCI-FI**
>
> Here's a particularly chilling take on biofuel: In the sci-fi classic The Matrix, robots take over Earth, but humans fight back by blocking out the Sun to cut off their solar power supply. The robots retaliate by turning humans into biofuel, imprisoning them in energy-harvesting pods that extract electricity from their bodies to power the machines.
>
> That's right—in The Matrix, humans are biofuels.
> As Keanu Reeves might say: Whoa.

GMO clostridium or E. coli bacteria. One potential problem: It may smell too much like bananas!

The world's population is more than 8 billion people, twice as many as 50 years ago, and could reach 9 billion by 2050. Yet the Earth itself is only so big, and many worry about how we will be able to meet the needs of this expanding population. Professor and ecologist Mike Berners-Lee estimates that demand for electricity will be seven times greater by 2100. If we cannot keep up with that, it could spell dire consequences for global civilization, including mass starvation. We will need new and better power resources, or use less energy in general—probably both. "Humanity is going to have to raise its game if it wants to take deliberate control over the amount of energy it uses," Berners-Lee writes in his book *There Is No Planet B*. There may be no perfect solution to the world's energy problems, but any improvement, even small, is better than not trying. We will need all the resources we can find, so biofuels, even if imperfect, are part of the solution.

Getting Real:

TRADITIONAL BIOFUELS

Biomass has been used as fuel for 100,000 years and still powers billions in the developing world. In many rural areas, wood remains the main source for cooking and heating, highlighting deep gaps in global energy access..

Approximately 2.5 billion people rely on traditional biomass such as wood, charcoal, crop residue, and dried animal dung, with 850 million in sub-Saharan Africa alone. An additional 300 million people use coal and kerosene. These fuels are not only time-consuming to gather but also pose serious health risks—indoor air pollution from burning them causes an estimated 3.8 million deaths annually due to respiratory diseases.

Charcoal is a particularly common fuel because it is compact, energy-dense, and easy to use—you might recognize it as the black, fist-sized briquettes used for backyard grilling. However, as demand grows, charcoal production contributes to deforestation, worsening environmental degradation.

Efforts have been made to develop cleaner, more efficient cooking stoves to reduce pollution and health risks. In the 1990s, China launched a major initiative to distribute 130 million improved stoves to rural households. However, many of these stoves were costly and complex to maintain, limiting widespread adoption. Solar-powered electric stoves could offer a long-term solution, but challenges remain in making them affordable and accessible to those who need them most.

BIOMASS POWER PLANTS

Although large-scale biomass power plants were slow to gain traction, they are now an important part of the global energy mix, with several facilities producing enough electricity to power entire regions.

For years, the largest biomass power plant in the world was Ironbridge in Shropshire, England. Originally a coal plant, it was converted to run entirely on wood pellets in 2013, reaching a 740-megawatt capacity before its closure in 2015.

Currently, the world's largest operational biomass plant is Alholmens Kraft Power Station in Pietarsaari, Finland. This massive facility runs primarily on tree bark, wood chips, logging byproducts, and peat. Every hour, it burns 800 cubic meters of biomass to heat the world's largest boiler, to produce steam to power three giant turbines. At full capacity, Alholmens Kraft generates 240 megawatts of electricity while also supplying steam and heat to local industries.

In the United States, over 600 biomass plants contribute about 1.2% of the nation's electricity supply. The largest, the 115-megawatt Nacogdoches Generating Facility in Sacul, Texas, is one of many plants helping to diversify America's energy sources.

As renewable energy demand grows, biomass power plants expand and help drive the shift away from fossil fuels.

Timeline

1826
Samuel Morey develops an early internal combustion engine powered by ethanol and turpentine.

1850s
Ethanol begins to be used as a lighting fuel in the United States

1900
Rudolf Diesel demonstrates his engine running on peanut oil at the World Exhibition in Paris, showcasing the potential of biofuels.

1925
Henry Ford predicts ethanol will be the "fuel of the future" and designs the Model T to run on ethanol.

1940s
During World War II, biofuels like ethanol are used as substitutes for gasoline due to shortages.

1970s
The oil crisis prompts renewed interest in biofuels, leading to increased ethanol production in Brazil and the United States.

1980s
Brazil launches its Proálcool program, making ethanol a major fuel source for vehicles.

1990s
Biodiesel production begins to expand in Europe, driven by environmental concerns and government incentives.

2005
The U.S. Energy Policy Act mandates the blending of renewable fuels like ethanol into gasoline.

2023
Bioethanol and biodiesel production reach 1,200 TWh, marking significant growth compared to 100 TWh in 1990.

Websites

Alholmens Kraft Power Plant
https://www.alholmenskraft.com/en/
Finland's largest biomass power station has a good website in English explaining how it works.

Visualizing Energy
https://visualizingenergy.org/
This project of the Boston University Institute for Global Sustainability presents data analysis and charts about energy, climate change, and health impacts of pollution.

Marine Agronomy
https://marineagronomy.org/
Explore the future of ocean seaweed farming at this site co-produced by the World Wildlife Fund and University of Hawaii.

Glossary

anaerobic — a process that takes place without oxygen

aquaculture — farming of aquatic plants and animals by humans for use as food, fuel, or other resources

bioenergy — energy, often electricity or heat, made using biomass or biofuels

biofuel — any fuel derived from biomass, which can be used for industry or personal human use as a replacement or

biomass — plant materials and animal waste used as a source of fuel.

carbon-neutrality — a goal for alternative energy that it should not put more of the greenhouse element carbon into the atmosphere than was required to harvest it.

fossil fuel — hydrocarbon fuels such as petroleum oil and gas made in the ancient past from biological sources and found in Earth's crust

greenhouse gas — gases such as carbon dioxide, methane, and water vapor which contribute to global warming by absorbing infrared radiation (heat) and reflecting it back to Earth's surface

global warming — a human-caused increase in worldwide air and ocean temperature

photosynthesis — the process by which green plants convert light into chemical energy to live and grow

renewability — a goal for alternative energy that it will never run out (such as sunlight and wind) or will replenish over time.

sustainability — a goal for alternative energy that it will not damage Earth's climate or humans' ability to harvest it.

watt — a unit of measurement defining how much energy must be expended to do a task, such as climbing a ladder or lighting a lightbulb

watt-hours — a unit of measurement used in power generation, defined as the energy made if one watt is generated for one hour

Selected Bibliography

Berners-Lee, Mike. *There Is No Planet B: A Handbook for the Make Or Break Years*. United States, Cambridge University Press, 2019.

Jacobson, Mark Z.. *No Miracles Needed: How Today's Technology Can Save Our Climate and Clean Our Air*. United Kingdom, Cambridge University Press, 2023.

Jelley, Nick. *Renewable Energy: A Very Short Introduction*. United Kingdom, OUP Oxford, 2020.

Jones, Jamie L.. *Rendered Obsolete: Energy Culture and the Afterlife of US Whaling*. United States: University of North Carolina Press, 2023.

McDonald, Bob. *The Future Is Now: Solving the Climate Crisis with Today's Technologies*. Canada, Penguin Canada, 2024.

Meier, Paul F., *The Changing Energy Mix: A Systematic Comparison of Renewable and Nonrenewable Energy* (New York, 2020; online edn, Oxford Academic, 18 Feb. 2021), https://doi-org.wikipedialibrary.idm.oclc.org/10.1093/oso/9780190098391.001.0001, accessed 29 Oct. 2024.

Rhodes, Richard. *Energy: A Human History*. United Kingdom: Simon & Schuster, 2019.

Simon, Christopher A.. *Alternative Energy: Political, Economic, and Social Feasibility*. United States, Rowman & Littlefield Publishers, 2020.

Index

Aeolipile (Hero of Alexandria), 22
anaerobic digestion, 15, 32
bio-jet fuel, 28, 32
biodiesel, 8, 16, 24, 28, 31, 32
biofuel feedstocks, 12, 40
biofuel generations, 16, 40
biomass, 12, 15, 27, 35, 39, 40, 44, 45
carbon Capture, 40
charcoal, 15, 18, 21, 44
deforestation, 21, 39, 45
ethanol, 8, 15, 21, 24, 25, 28, 31, 42
fermentation, 15, 21, 27
genetic modification, 42
green crude, 42
land use, 16, 21
landfill gas capture, 31
methane, 15, 27, 31, 32, 34
palm oil industry, 22, 39
photosynthesis, 12, 35
Rudolf Diesel, 22
seaweed, 38, 42
sugarcane ethanol, 24
switchgrass, 12, 40
thermal conversion, 15
whale oil, 22
wood pellets, 17, 28, 45